HYDE PARK

IN ITS GLORY

HYDE PARK
IN ITS GLORY

An Historical Sketch

By the
Hyde Park Business Club
JULY, 1908

Originally published by the Hyde Park Business Club in 1908
© Copyright 2021 by Commonwealth Book Company, St. Martin, Ohio

ISBN: 978-1-948986-37-3

To the People of Hyde Park
This Volume is Dedicated
by the Committee.

HYDE PARK ENGINE HOUSE

Erected by Chas. Rosenstiel & Son
Contractors, Builders and Manufacturers of Millwork
Cincinnati, Ohio

Harry Hake, Architect.

DEDICATION OF THE NEW ENGINE HOUSE

... BY ...

THE HYDE PARK BUSINESS CLUB

... AND ...

CITIZENS OF HYDE PARK

July 18th, 1908, Commencing at 4 o'clock P. M.

Reception for the Ladies at the New Engine House 2:30 to 4 P. M.

The Hyde Park Business Club Committee on Engine House
Dedication Ceremonies

JAS. L. ANSPAUGH	Chairman
W. J. TAYLOR	Vice Chairman
JAS. C. GREGSON	Secretary
MYERS Y. COOPER	
L. E. ZIEGLE	

PROGRAM

Dedication Ceremonies

Auditorium, Hyde Park Town Hall, 4 P. M.

Hon. L. E. Ziegle, Presiding

Music, ...	By Band
Chorus, ...	The Hyde Park Children
Presentation of Flag, . . .	Mr. Myers Y. Cooper
Acceptance of Flag, . . .	Hon. Wm. F. Boyd, President Board of Public Safety
Chorus "Star Spangled Banner," .	The Hyde Park Children
Music, ...	By Band
Chorus, ...	The Hyde Park Children
Music, ...	By Band

General Flag Display on the part of Citizens, in the Decoration of their Homes.

Hourly Cannon Salutes from Sunrise to Sunset.

Grand Fireworks Display 8 to 9 P. M.

Cannon and Fireworks Display in charge of Mr. Chris. Stichnath.

BANQUET

...OF...

THE HYDE PARK BUSINESS CLUB

DEDICATION OF THE ENGINE HOUSE

...AT THE...

TOWN HALL, SATURDAY, JULY 18th, 1908
7.30 P. M.

MENU.

BOUILLON

CANOPIES   CRACKERS   PICKLES   OLIVES

FILET SOLE   TARTAR SAUCE   POTATO BALLS

BROILED CHICKEN

PEAS   SHERBET

LETTUCE, TOMATO AND CUCUMBER

WHITE ROCK

NEAPOLITAN ICE CREAM

CAKES   FRUIT

COFFEE

ROQUEFORT CHEESE   BENT CRACKERS

CIGARS

PROGRAM

Toastmaster . . . Hon. W. C. Culkins
President Hyde Park Business Club

City of Cincinnati . . Hon. Leopold Markbreit
Mayor of Cincinnati

Hyde Park . . . Hon. Wallace Burch

Board of Public Safety . . Hon. Wm. F. Boyd

Board of Public Service . Hon. Robt. Laidlaw

City of Norwood . . . Hon. Charles Herbert Jones
Mayor of Norwood

Address . . . Hon. M. E. Ingalls

HISTORY OF THE HYDE PARK BUSINESS CLUB

THE Hyde Park Business Club is the lineal descendent of the Madison Road Improvement Association, which was organized to obtain better street car facilities, particularly on the Oakley line. It met in the offices of the Hyde Park Lumber Company. Development of that section in the vicinity of the Public Square naturally led to the removal of the organization to a more central location and a change of the name to Hyde Park Improvement Association. Both of these organizations were extremely active and obtained many important improvements. In the Fall of 1906 it was decided to enlarge the scope of the Association and it was reorganized into the Hyde Park Business Club.

This body took up the unfinished work of its predecessors and set about accomplishing things in the way of adding to the comfort and convenience as well as the entertainment of the people of Hyde Park, and the general uplift of this delightful section. Owing to the great increase in population and the number of frame structures erected, a special effort was made to obtain suitable fire protection and it was through the organized effort of the club that this was brought about. Many other improvements were obtained. A Branch Library, High School, additional Educational Facilities, Parks, Playgrounds, Boulevards and improved streets are in contemplation. The Federated Improvement Association, which forms a central body for all of the organizations of a similar character, was brought about by a resolution of the Hyde Park Business Club. It has taken an active part in general improvements, such as a Greater Park System, the Annexation League, the Improvement of the Canal, the Gilbert Avenue Viaduct, etc.

It must not be inferred that the splendid public building of the fire companies is the only thing actually brought about. There is not a resident of this section who cannot see the steady forward movement of the suburb under the co-operative influence of the club with its subdivisions of labor among the hustling committees.

The street car service has been vastly improved. The incandescent illumination of streets makes it easily the best lighted suburb in Cincinnati. The beautification of the public square and the improvements on the thoroughfares within and leading to Hyde Park are forerunners of the greater things which are to follow.

Lectures and other entertainments, to which all of the residents of the section are invited whether or not members of the club, have been held with great sucess.

There is no organization of its kind in the city which receives such cordial support from all the people benefitted as the Hyde Park Business Club, and this is testified to by the fact that its membership roll is 500; which easily surpasses all others.

Many additional projects for the benefit of this section are under consideration. Among these are the Branch Library, the extension of Observatory Avenue to Woodburn Avenue, and eventually across the city to the canal west of Clifton, a Viaduct connecting Hyde Park with Evanston, bringing the two neighborly sections within walking distance, the development of a Cross Town line which will connect all of the suburbs lying in the outer residence zone of the city and including Norwood, rapid transit facilities to the business section of the city, the annexation of territory which will make Madisonville contiguous to the city, the erection of a suitable Auditorium and Club House with Gymnasium, the extension of Erie Avenue and other streets to afford additional opportunities for the home seekers attracted to this popular section, and the general betterment of the street sewer and transportation conditions.

With these and other plans under way it is reasonably certain that the club membership will in the near future reach one thousand, with all that means in way of influence and united effort for development, beautification and mutual betterment of conditions already superior to those found in other sections of QUEEN OF THE WEST.

OFFICERS
1906-1907

President - - - - LOUIS E. ZIEGLE
First Vice-Pres. - ALBERT O. KRAEMER
Second Vice-Pres. - - LOUIS H. BOLCE
Recording Sec. - MARTIN H. SCHUBELER
Corresponding Sec. - EDMUND G. COOK
Treasurer - - - - ALBERT ERKINS

DIRECTORS

DR. R. W. C. FRANCIS   FRANK H. KINNEY
ANDREW P. HENKEL   A. G. RIST
ELDON R. JAMES   CHRIS. STICHNATH
L. L. SADLER

OFFICERS
1907-1908

President - - - - WM. C. CULKINS
First Vice-Pres. - - - FRANK O. SUIRE
Second Vice-Pres. - - HERBERT T. KENT
Recording Sec. - MARTIN H. SCHUBELER
Corresponding Sec. - - - M. J. FLYNN
Treasurer - - - - EDMUND G. COOK

DIRECTORS

LOUIS H. BOLCE   L. L. SADDLER
DR. A. L. BROWN   CHRIS. STICHNATH
FRANK H. KINNEY   R. B. TODD
LOUIS E. ZIEGLE

Top Row Left to Right: J. L. Anspaugh, Dr. Arthur L. Brown, A. C. Volkman, M. J. Flynn, C. Harvey Witte, R. B. Todd, M. F. Galvin. Second Row: J. C. Gregson, J. Gano Wright, Edmund Cook, R. E. Morrison, Dr. R. W. C. Francis, M. Y. Cooper, Luke Smith. Third Row: J. A. Bolser, F. H. Kinney, M. H. Schubeler, H. T. Kent, W. C. Culkins, Chris. Stichnath, Louis Bolce.

Hon. L. E. Ziegle, 1st Pres. of Club

Hon. W. C. Culkins, 2nd Pres. of Club

HYDE PARK TOWN HALL

...Meeting Place of the...

Hyde Park Business Club

Hyde Park Lodge No. 589 F. & A. M.

Hyde Park National Union

Hyde Park Independent Order of Foresters

Hyde Park Methodist Church, (Temporary)

COMMITTEES

In Each Committee, the First Mentioned Name is that of the Chairman.

LEGISLATION
W. S. Little, F. L. Hoffman, Wm. Littleford, L. D. Oliver, Simeon M. Johnson.

STREETS AND SEWERS
A. G. Rist, C. Stichnath, W. C. Kohlhoff, Anthony Koars, Sam'l Greatorex.

FIRE DEPARTMENT
M. Y. Cooper, A. P. Henkel, J. Q. Martin, J. G. Penn, T. W. Spalding.

PARKS, PLAY-GROUNDS AND BEAUTIFICATION
F. H. Youmans, A. O. Kraemer, H. E. Stagman, Al. Dietrich, Raphael Pedretti.

POLICE
J. R. Jacobs, B. S. Wydman, Gustave Hinnau, A. Erkins, A. E. Heekin.

SANITATION
Dr. C. M. Paul, Dr. Charles Weber, Dr. E. Cundell Juler, Dr. F. M. Oxley, Dr. Ralph Reed.

WATER SUPPLY
H. L. Ottenjohn, Walter L. Griest, George Mellor, A. J. Murphy, M. Snowden.

SIDEWALKS
M. F. Galvin, J. R. Jordan, Frank Wilson, Charles Garber, H. Zering.

STREET RAILROAD
L. E. Ziegle, Robert Weinheimer, H. F. Bachmeyer, Wimot J. Hall, J. A. Seymour.

ELEVATED RAILROAD
J. Gano Wright, C. A. Eberle, J. M. Sundmaker, A. E. DeArmond, L. D. Sargent.

ANNEXATION
C. H. Jenkins, J. C. Frohliger, Frank Lewis, Joseph Sanger, D. M. Martin.

PUBLICITY
R. E. Morrison, W. J. Taylor, R. B. Bowman, Harvey C. Witte, M J. Flynn.

COMMITTEES

VIADUCTS
J. A. Bolser, John Zettle, A. A. Andridge, L. G. Blair, W. E. Richards.

STREET SPRINKLING
A. L. Fahnestock, T. F. Dickinson, C. L. Cox, G. L. Wright.

BRANCH LIBRARY
L. L. Sadler, J. C. Gregson, E. J. Stahl, J. H. Zeiner, A. J. Becht.

SCHOOLS
Bryant Venable, Malcolm McAvoy, A. C. Volkman, O. R. Bohache, W. J. Rohr.

GAS AND ELECTRICITY
Dr. R. W. C. Francis, A. E. Rowley, W. B. Carpenter, J. H. Spellmire, Daniel Desmond.

EXTENSION OF OBSERVATORY AVE.
G. F. Osler, A. B. Horton, Herbert T. Kent, R. B. Cadwalader, G. J. Boedker.

ENTERTAINMENT
J. C. Gregson, Luke W. Smith, Dr. A. L. Brown, E. R. James, A. B. Horton.

GRADE CROSSINGS
F. H. Kinney, Edward Shannon, F. J. Lingo, Harvey Witte, E. B. Grabow.

DELEGATES TO FEDERATED IMPROVEMENT ASS'N
W. C. Culkins, F. H. Kinney, Eldon R. James.

POSTAL SERVICE
Edmund G. Cook, Otto E. Betz, John J. Porter, E. C. Cordes, Dr. A. A. Kumler.

CONSTITUTION AND ROSTER
Luke W. Smith, Eldon R. James, Andrew P. Henkel.

MEMBERSHIP
L. D. Sargent, W. W. Widmeyer, Arthur L. Betts, C. D. Millar, Dr. J. L. McLeish.

List of Members

Name.	Residence.
Argo, W. A.	2712 Oakley Ave.
Atwood, Earnest T.	1551 St. Leger Pl., E. W. H.
Asbury, Frank C.	2622 Madison Rd.
Angebrandt, Arthur E.	2925 Observatory Ave.
Anspaugh, J. L.	2819 Erie Ave.
Andridge, A. A.	1317 Grace Ave.
Archiable, R. J. H.	3825 Drake Ave.
Altomare, W. E.	2816 Observatory Ave.
Archiable, Geo. W.	3542 Michigan Ave.
Allison, James	Betz Bldg., H. P.
Allison, Jas	House of Refuge.
Applegate, Frank	3006 Paxton Rd.
Allen, Clyde M.	3322 Monteith Ave.
Andrew, Robert	3600 Shaw Ave.
Andrew, Frank M.	3600 Shaw Ave.
Allen, James B.	3950 Edwards Rd.
Ankenbauer, John F.	2839 Observatory Ave.
Atwood, John K.	1551 St. Leger Pl., E. W. H.
Ahrens, W. A. Sr.	3523 Mooney Ave.
Avey, F. H.	2822 Erie Ave.
Beahr, Major	Ruth Ave., E. W. H.
Bigler, C. W.	Edwards Rd.
Brookfield, Carroll	3551 Mooney Ave.
Baker, Will E.	2721 Oakley Ave.
Brown, Dr. Arthur L.	2637 Erie Ave.
Behymer, Arthur L.	3435 Observatory Pl.
Broadwell, Charles	2718 Wasson Rd.
Boedker, G. J.	2775 Observatory Ave.
Buchanan, G. H.	Linwood nr. Observatory
Ballauf, Louis G.	3535 Mooney Ave.
Brown, Frank R.	2815 Observatory Ave.
Brutton, Harry L.	3531 Monteith Ave.
Bolce, Wm. A.	N. W. Cor. Belmont & Ivy
Blowney, B. C.	2486 Observatory Ave.
Bland, John	Edwards Rd., Sta. O.
Betz, Otto E.	S. W. Cor. Erie & Edwards
Bachmeyer, H. F.	3518 St. Charles Pl.
Brockhoff, Julius A.	3532 Monteith Ave.
Betts, Arthur L.	3515 Shaw Ave.
Barr, Wm. B.	Ferris Ave., W. of Delta
Bolser, Joseph A.	Fairview & Ivy Ave.
Bolce, Louis W.	Fairview & Ivy Ave.
Bolce, Henry B.	Fairview & Ivy Ave.
Bolce, Louis H.	Fairview & Ivy Ave.
Bohache, O. R.	Madison Rd. & Erie Ave.
Bliss, R. C.	3527 Monteith Ave.
Bott, John F.	Herschel Ave.
Blair, L. G.	3825 Mt. Vernon Ave.
Bowman, R. B.	2973 Observatory Ave.
Baumann, John A.	3570 Michigan Ave.
Bolce, Henry	1981 Madison Rd.
Becht, A. J.	3283 Red Bank Ave.
Brown, Geo. M.	3557 Edwards Rd.
Benckenstein, J. J.	2634 Madison Rd.
Brooks, Chas. W.	Mt. Vernon Ave.
Burkhold, Henry	2634 Erie Ave.
Burkholz, Edward	2825 Erie Ave.
Buchanan, Geo. M.	3822 Millsbrae Ave.
Burch, Wallace M.	2805 Madison Rd.
Beyer, Geo.	3754 Mt. Vernon Ave.
Bruner, Simon	2642 Stanton Ave., W. H.
Bode, L. E.	3815 Fairview Ave.
Bingham, Wm.	Madison Rd.
Beckel, Geo.	Grace Ave.
Brown, W. L.	2824 Erie Ave.
Brown, E.	3805 McCormick Rd.
Cutler, Poe A.	3765 Mt. Vernon Ave.
Crane, E. J.	3766 Mt. Vernon Ave.
Casello, Dr. J. B.	4 E. 9th St., Cincinnati
Cadwalader, Richard B.	3438 Fairview Ave.
Cryer, Frank	1335 Paxton Ave.
Cook, Edmund G	3521 Fairview Ave.
Carpenter, C. C.	Alaise Bldg.
Carpenter, W B	Alaise Bldg.
Culkins, Wm. C.	3414 Monteith Ave.
Cannon, I. J.	3559 Shaw Ave.
Cadwalader, Peirce J.	3438 Fairview Ave.
Cunny, Louis S.	2815 Observatory Ave.
Courtright, Dr. J. L.	Cor. Erie & Edwards
Cox, Clarence L.	3536 Zumstein Ave.
Calkins, G. W.	2864 Wasson Rd.
Culver, C. J.	856 Lincoln Ave.
Culver, Geo. C.	2728 Mitchell Ave.
Clark, Albert Meyers	Clark & Observatory Aves.
Cordes, Ed. C.	2714 Wasson Rd.
Cordes, Emil	3524 Edwards Rd.
Cutler, O. J.	3637 Edwards Rd.
Crim, Cal.	2378 Menlo Ave.
Cooper, M. Y.	3590 Mooney Ave.
Cohen, Edward A	2724 Mitchell Ave.
Clemons, W. H	2623 Erie Ave.
Cooper, Dr. W. A	3721 Woodland Ave.
Comer, Walter	2678 Madison Ave.
Culver, C. J.	2863 Erie Ave.
Davidson, W. J.	2613 Observatory Ave.
Dickinson, Dr. T. F.	2551 Erie Ave.
Diehl, Francis F.	3539 Shaw Ave.
Dixon, Earnest	Madison Ave.
Dunlap, B. J.	3567 Edwards Rd.
Drainie, John G.	3546 Shaw Ave.
Drapp, Edward	2461 Madison Road
Dickens, Henry	3770 Drake Ave.
Duncan, James H.	Clark & Observatory Aves.
Dietz, John	2916 Portsmouth Ave.
Dietrich, Albert	3615 Edwards Rd.
Drake, F. B.	3719 Portland Ave.
Drake, C. W.	3019 Paxton Ave.
Dyer, F. B.	Burch Ave.
DeMoller, Jr., John	3735 Woodland Ave.
Defosse, Chas.	Park & Yale Ave., W H.
Desmond, Daniel	3835 McCormick Rd.
Deutschele, Jos.	2722 Oakley Ave.
Douglas, W. W.	2924 Cleinview Ave., W. H.
DeArmond, A. E.	3425 Stettinius Ave.

List of Members—Continued.

Name.	Residence.
Edwards, J. R.	3628 Michigan Ave.
Eberle, Chas. A.	2843 Observatory Ave.
Evans, Thos	3515 Mooney Ave.
Eilers, John	3624 Edwards Rd.
Eichhorn, Edw. Ch.	3653 Michigan Ave.
Evers, Wm	2920 Madison Rd.
Elliott, Geo. T	3818 Drake Ave.
Erkins, Albert	Burch Ave.
Erbacher, E. F.	Wasson & Paxton Rds.
Flynn, Michael J.	3428 Monteith Ave.
Freeman, S. H	2815 Oakley Ave.
Forder, Alfred	E. Walnut Hills
Fahnestock, A. L.	3001 Observatory Ave.
Fahnestock, L. W.	3001 Observatory Ave.
French, A. S.	2444 Observatory Ave.
Fishwick, A. B.	2654 Madison Rd.
Foertmeyer, A. W.	City Hospital.
Fox, Frank	2845 Astoria Ave.
Ford, Warren W	3606 Edwards Rd.
Francis, Dr. Robin W. C.	2767 Madison Rd.
Fryer, W. B.	2863 Erie Ave.
Frohliger, John C.	3504 Erie Ave.
Fagel, Chas. H	2930 Portsmouth Ave.
French, Tilden R	2448 Observatory Ave.
Foertmeyer, A. W.	Edwards Rd.
Ferris, E. E.	4809 Morse St.
Foy, Wm. F.	3439 Berry Ave.
Fehl, C. D.	3518 Handman Ave.
Foley, Prof. B. W.	2546 Observatory Ave.
Fagin, Jos. T	1112 St. Gregory St.
Ginsler, Theo. J.	1822 Hewitt Ave.
Glenn, John Q.	3906 Edwards Rd.
Goelitz, H	Delta Ave., Sta. O.
Grimes, J. C.	3726 Woodland Ave.
Ginter, G. A.	3641 Edwards Rd.
Griest, W. H.	3257 Observatory Ave.
Garlick, Henry	Erie & Mooney Ave.
Geisler, Theo. J.	3571 Zumstein Ave.
Grote, C. L.	2008 Madison Rd.
Grote, Fred	2008 Madison Rd.
Greaves, Wm. A	3525 Michigan Ave.
Green, G.	1219 Grace Ave.
Galvin, M. F.	3443 Stettinius Ave.
Givens, A. D.	3561 Edwards Rd.
Grabow, Emil B	3710 Oakley Ave.
Griest, Edwin L.	3257 Observatory Ave.
Gilbert, B. L.	3637 Edwards Rd.
Garber, Charles	3834 Millsbrae Ave.
Gruber, Wm. D.	2880 Linwood Rd.
Gores, Guido	Hackberry & Fernwood
Goodwin, Frank P.	3435 Observatory Pl.
Greatorex, Samuel	Rex Place
Gregson, James C.	3622 Zumstein Ave.
Goldkamp, Albert	2245 Ivy Ave.
Getker, W. C.	3014 Wasson Rd.
Gillespie, Michael	Shaw & Rochelle Ave.
Goelitz, H.	2828 Erie Ave.
Gauspohl, Edw.	**3610 Zumstein Ave.**

Name.	Residence.
George, T. Benj.	2729 Oakley Ave.
Guiney, Ed	2876 Erie Ave.
Greenwald, C. E.	3562 Zumstein Ave.
Gill, W. C.	No. 9, St. Leger Bldg., W. H.
Gates, Harry L.	Edwards Rd.
Goelitz, A	Red Bank Ave.
Heiselmann, Frank	3834 Edwards Rd.
Hart, John S.	3520 Mooney Ave.
Hood, Frank M	3551 Michigan Ave.
Holden, E. G.	3535 Zumstein Ave.
Hartsough, H. W.	Cleneay & Spencer, Nor.
Hagans, Elisha M.	1338 Meier Ave.
Hubbell, John M.	3437 Stettinius Ave.
Honer, Albert P.	3625 Michigan Ave.
Handman, C. W.	3621 Morris Place
Henkel, Paul L.	Erie & Mooney Aves.
Henkel, Andrew P	Erie & Mooney Aves.
Harvey, W. L.	1320 Grace Ave.
Holley, W. D.	3892 Isabella Ave.
Hollingsworth, Fred W.	Monteith Ave.
Horton, A. Bart.	1315 Grace Ave.
Hall, Wilmot J.	3605 Shaw Ave.
Hoffman, Fred L.	2719 Madison Rd.
Horton, A. C.	Betz Flats
Howland, D. B.	Mt. Airy, Sta. K.
Heekin, Albert E.	3528 Mooney Ave.
Hinnau, Gustav.	3742 Woodland Ave.
Hoffman, J. H.	3542 Michigan Ave.
Helmers, Albert	3634 Zumstein Ave.
Heckman, John B.	Betz Bldg.
Henkel, Roy G.	3566 Edwards Rd.
Hynes, Rev. P. J.	Ashmont & Shady Lane
Heinrichsdorf, Geo. C.	2875 Erie Ave.
Huls, J. E.	2119 Woodland, E. W. H.
Howland, D. B.	Monteith Flats, H. P.
Harris, J. M.	3803 Hazel Ave., Nor. O.
Hennessy, Edw. J.	Edwards & Mitchell Aves.
Herrlinger, John	3615 Shaw Ave.
Huls, J. E.	Mt. Washington, O.
Huser, Edw.	3244 Gilbert Ave.
Hardig, J. Peter	Dixon & Halstead St.
Huber, Joseph	3567 Zumstein Ave.
Irvine, John W.	3758 Oakley Ave.
Isham, Charles C.	3458 Observatory Pl.
James, Eldon R.	2826 Erie Ave.
Jenny, John H. Jr.	3661 Michigan Ave.
Jones, E. Lawrence	2885 Linwood Rd.
Jeffers, R. A.	3520 St. Charles Pl.
Johnson, Simeon M.	3427 Burch Ave.
Juler, Edward Cundell	2854 Erie Ave.
Jones, Edward C.	3552 Edwards Road
Jordan, James R.	3731 Drake Avenue
Jenkins, C. H.	2806 Madison Rd.
Jenny, John H., Jr.	3751 Union Ave.
Jacobs, John R.	3515 St. Charles Pl.
Jahnke, William	2926 Portsmouth Ave.
James, Thomas	Alexandra Flat, No. 6
Janowitz, F. J	**3630 Edwards Rd.**

List of Members—Continued.

Name.	Residence.	Name.	Residence.
Jacob, W. H.	2526 Madison Ave.	Martin, J. Q.	3763 Mt. Vernon
Janzen, Geo.	Oakley & Madison Ave.	Maurer, Geo. E	3776 Drake Ave.
Jones, Robert D.	Edwards Rd.	McCord, Frank Lincoln	2735 Madison Ave.
Jordon, Geo	Paxton & Wasson Rds.	Martin, C. DeLaney	3838 Millsbrae Ave.
Kraemer, Albert O	2816 Erie Ave.	Martin, Daniel W	2208 Spring Grove Ave.
Kaiser, Otto	2961 Madison Rd.	Mellor, Edward F	3424 Walworth Ave.
King, Dr. J. R.	2648 Erie Ave.	Millar, Claude Davis	2430 Observatory Ave.
Kolb, Louis	3418 Monteith Ave.	Mehlhope, John F	3711 Union Ave.
Keller, Gustav	3730 Woodland Ave.	Messerschmitt, Charles	3546 Shaw Ave.
Kramer, Henry W	3302 Monteith Ave.	Metz, Daniel	2648 Melrose Ave., W. H.
Kinney, Joel F	3600 Mooney Ave.	Metz, Phil	3523 Monteith Ave.
Kerans, Wm.	Menlo Ave. Station O.	Maurer, George	3815 Mt. Vernon Ave.
Kellogg, Edwin E	3807 Eastern Ave.	Matlack, H. C.	2750 Erie Ave.
Koars, Anthony	1360 Herschel Ave.	Metz, James F	3523 Monteith Ave.
Keck, Emanuel V	Isabella and Paxton Rd.	Morrison, R. E.	3516 Michigan Ave.
Kuhn, Walter W	3417 Burch Ave.	Miller, John R	3551 Shaw Ave.
Kreimer, August G	Erie & Duncan.	Molloy, Harry	2716 Arbor Ave.
Kent, Herbert T	3555 Shaw Ave.	Morton, Chas. H	318 E. 2nd St.
Klayer, Fred W	3775 Drake Ave.	McBreen, James	3620 Edwards Rd.
Kohlhoff, Wm. C	2836 Erie Ave.	McAvoy, Malcolm	Observatory, Cor. Berry.
Kinney, J W	3906 Edwards Rd.	Massmann, Albert W	4637 Smith Road, Nor. O.
Kinney, Frank H	3633 Zumstein Ave.	Matthews, S. C.	3531 Zumstein Ave.
Kruse, Wm. A	3580 Mooney Ave.	McLeish, Dr. John Lewin	2615 Erie Ave.
Knowles, F. A	3806 Oakley Ave.	Murphy, Andrew J	3752 Mt. Vernon Ave.
Kaiser, Louis H	2713 Euclid Ave.	Miller, James Albert	2611 Southside Ave.
Kreuter, Chas. W	2720 Oakley Ave.	Merkhofer, Arthur	3938 Catherine, Nor., O.
Koehler, Fred, Jr.	3563 Mooney Ave.	Marshall, Howard	Mitchell St.
Kahoe, Michael	3738 Woodland Ave.	Mahoney, J	3714 Oakley Ave.
Keyler, Chas. W	Wabash Ave.	Metcalfe, E. P.	3635 Edwards Rd.
Kelsch, Harry	3820 Mt. Vernon Ave.	Merpall, O. F.	Mooney Ave.
Klohr, Jno. N	3568 Zumstein Ave.	Menzel, Leonard	2714 Mitchell Ave.
Kadow, Wm.	2850 Minto Ave.	Moore, Richard H.	947 McMillan St.
Kyle, William	2827 Observatory Ave.	Mohrhoff, August	2921 Portsmouth Ave.
Lane, Geo A	Kemper & Central Aves.	Mellor, Geo. L	3611 Shaw Ave.
Loth, George P	3512 Monteith Ave.	Merrell, C. G	2472 Observatory Ave.
Leahy, Dr. D. A	3530 Shaw Ave.	Merrell, Stanley W	2462 Observatory Ave.
Lutz, Thomas	2893 Williams Ave.	Millar, H. M.	2430 Observatory Ave.
Lodder, Fred J	3816 Edwards Rd.	Moarn, Jas.	Newton, O.
Leeds, Dr. H. Nelson	Observatory Ave.	McCord, Frank	2735 Madison Rd.
Littleford, Hon. Wm	2521 Salem Ave.	Miller, Dr. J. R.	2840 Observatory Ave.
Little, W. S.	2941 Observatory Ave.	Miller, John R	3551 Shaw Ave.
Littleford, Hon. Wm	1st. Nat. Bank Bldg.	Meyer, John H	2664 Madison Rd.
Lawrence, Albert	3450 Burch Ave.	Martin, Daniel W	3729 Drake Ave.
Leighton, Geo. J	3739 Woodland Ave.	McDonald, Jas. J.	2839 Observatory Ave.
Lockhorn, Chas. E	3447 Burch Ave.	McGuire, N. S	3733 Mt. Vernon Ave.
Lingonner, Fred H	3742 Oakley Ave.	McConn, Clarence	3721 Woodland Ave.
Lahusen, George	3584 Zumstein Ave.	McDonald, Edward	2995 Observatory Ave.
Lewis, Frank	Marion & Union Aves.	McCarren, Geo.	Edwards & Williams.
Legnor, John W	3553 Edwards Rd.	Nevin, Louis G	3916 Edwards Rd.
Lingonner, Geo. A	2689 Madison Rd.	Nichol, Thos. J	3413 Burch Ave.
Lane, Geo. A	Flat F, Betz Flats, H. P.	Nayler, John	2899 Williams Ave.
Lockhorn, Geo.	3447 Burch Ave.	Netzer, David	305 Com. Trib. Bldg.
Lens, Henry F	3892 Isabella St.	Nurre, J. M.	3443 Burch Ave.
Lee, Robt. E	2619 Melrose Ave.	Neave, Jos. S	2243 Grandin Rd.
Lingo, F. J	3744 Portland Ave.	O'Connell, Hon. Jno. G	1325 Grace Ave.
Lans, Al. V	2875 Williams Ave.	Oliver, L. D	3544 Mooney Ave.
Morton, Charles H	2633 Erie Ave.	Oxley, Dr. Francis Marion	3520 Edwards Rd.
Muchmore, Carl. W	Arbor Ave.	Orton, C. J	2863 Erie Ave.

List of Members—Continued.

Name.	Residence.
Ottenjohn, Henry L.	3552 Mooney Ave.
O'Brein, G. T.	17 Glengariff Bldg., W. H.
Osler, Hon. G. F.	1333 Grace Ave.
Oesper, Jr., E. Wm.	1527 Hapsburg St.
Piper, Robert N.	3807 Edwards Rd.
Paul, Dr. Charles M.	3526 Mooney Ave.
Pfeiffer, John N.	S. W. Cor. Obser. & Menlo.
Phillips, Dr. P. K.	2641 Erie Ave.
Pedretti, Raphael	"Montebello," H. P.
Pernice, Marion L.	3528 Monteith Ave.
Porter, John J.	3441 Observatory Pl.
Prinzbach, George A.	2817 Erie Ave.
Powers, H. H.	1646 Brewster Ave.
Poolger, Jos. P.	Zumstein Ave.
Pohl, Oscar	3735 Union Ave.
Pottschmid, Wm.	Observatory Ave.
Penn, Julius G.	1210 Halpin St.
Pool, James	Monteith Ave.
Patton, C. E.	3000 Paxton Ave.
Proctor, R. W.	2500 Observatory Ave.
Picard, Edwin T.	
Picard, Edward F.	3879 Isabella Ave.
Pfeiffer, Jno. N.	2841 Woodburn Ave.
Pister, Chas.	Mooney Ave.
Perkins, Lewis W.	3459 Observatory Ave.
Rieckelman, Edward J.	3606 Michigan Ave.
Rademacher, Wm. Henry	3860 Oakley Ave.
Reed, Dr. Ralph	2633 Erie Ave.
Rennemeier, Henry C.	2717 Oakley Ave.
Reed, Dr. Ralph	1414 Elm. St.
Richards, Warren E.	2805 Madison Rd.
Raisbeck, John E.	Cor. Monteith & Erie
Rau, G. Max	3334 Monteith Ave.
Ricker, Dr. Jos. W.	2719 Observatory Ave.
Redler, L.	2533 Erie Ave.
Roche, M. J.	3311 West Side Ave.
Rowley, A. E.	2837 Observatory Ave.
Rhodes, J. H.	3528 Zumstein Ave.
Reif, Edwards A.	2596 Madison Rd.
Roose, Leaman Christy	3549 Edwards Rd.
Roche, S. J.	2978 Paxton Rd.
Rofelty, Clarence J.	No. 5, Virginia Flats, H. P.
Rosenstiel, Matt E.	3621 Michigan Ave.
Ray, M. D., Victor	3584 Mooney Ave.
Rist, Anthony G.	2920 Madison Ave.
Runyan, Norman S.	2753 Observatory Ave.
Rohr, Will J.	3910 Edwards Rd.
Runyan, A. C.	2753 Observatory Ave.
Reuscher, A. L.	Erie & Michigan Aves.
Rugg, E. W.	Madison Ave.
Robinson, Geo. W.	1103 Delta Ave.
Roden, Earnest A.	3781 Oakley Ave.
Rau, H. Wm.	3611 Zumstein Ave.
Rickelman, F.	3606 Michigan Ave.
Ryan, Albert J.	3578 Zumstein Ave.
Reeves, Clif. B.	Salem Ave.
Rugg, Jos. K.	2658 Madison Rd.
Rheinhart, S.	Edwards & Wabash Ave.
Sachs, S. B.	824 Hutchins Ave., Avon.
Shannon, Edward	Burch Bldg., H. P.
Stagman, H. E.	2721 Oakley Ave.
Scheiffele, Wm. H.	3519 Mooney Ave.
Schmit, Chas. W.	2400 Madison Rd.
Sadler, L. L.	2500 Observatory Rd.
Smith, Luke W.	3457 Observatory Pl.
Stedman, Arthur	Menlo Ave., H, P.
Shafer, O. J.	2808 Erie Ave.
Snowden, Melville	3335 Monteith Ave.
Sullivan, Edward J	2841 Observatory Ave.
Stoehr, R. A.	Mt. Washington, O.
Schopper, Fred D.	3771 Millsbrae Ave.
Sullivan, John E.	2339 Park Ave., W. H.
Stiess, Wm. C.	1358 Grace Ave.
Schoelwer, W. H.	3574 Edwards Rd.
Saxby, Wm. Steer	3771 Oakley Ave.
Sokup, John B.	N. W. Cor. Erie & Mooney.
Spalding, T. W.	2558 Madison Rd.
Stansbury, Dr. F. R.	Marion & Isabella Sts.
Shearer, Robt. Moore	2619 Observatory Ave.
Stacey, Richard	3731 Oakley Ave.
Schneider, Prof. Geo. C.	3631 Michigan Ave.
Suire, Frank O.	3427 Berry Ave.
Schroder, J. B.	3521 Zumstein Ave.
Sanger, Joe	2819 Observatory Ave.
Sherwood, James E.	1337 Grace Ave.
Stall, Edward J.	2567 Erie Ave.
Stevens, Chas. A.	3627 Edwards Rd.
Smith, H. C.	2935 Observatory Ave.
Small, J. C.	3612 Zumstein Ave.
Schubeler, M. H.	3624 Edwards Rd.
Springmeier, Ferd	2812 Erie Ave.
Schmid, Chas. C.	Edwards & Wasson Rds.
Seilkop, H. H.	2881 Williams Ave.
Stanley, E. B.	2540 Madison Rd.
Striker, John	3603 Zumstein Ave.
Scollan, John	2647 Observatory Ave.
Schacht, Wm.	3626 Zumstein Ave.
Spellmire, J. H.	3482 Observatory Ave.
Stichnath, Chris.	3519 Shaw Ave.
Schenk, Michael	Erie & Paxton Rd.
Seymour, J. A	2948 Madison Rd.
Striker, Chas.	3630 Zumstein Ave.
Schoelwer, Henry	1204 Eden Park Court.
Sundmaker	3441 Stettinius Ave.
Seyfforle, Wm.	3753 Union Ave.
Scollan, Edw.	2647 Observatory Ave.
Setker, W. I.	1322 Chapel St.
Sullivan, G. W.	3543 Shaw Ave.
Shuff, John L.	Hotel Alms, W. H.
Shaw, H. F.	3428 Stettinius Ave.
Sullivan, E. W.	3815 Isabella Ave.
Shaw, H. C.	3428 Stettinius Ave.
Sargent, L. D.	3527 Zumstein Ave.
Snyder, G. W.	2609 Southside Ave.
Tully, E. J.	2841 Station Ave., W. H.
Treudley, Harry B.	3860 Oakley Ave.

List of Members—Continued.

Name.	Residence.
Turner, William Henry	3645 Edwards Rd.
Treudley, T. F.	3842 Millsbrae Ave.
Todd, R. B.	3430 Burch Ave.
Tauber, A.	3704 Oakley Ave.
Taylor, W. J.	2728 Erie Ave.
Treudley, H. A.	3830 Millsbrae Ave.
Tietig, Rudolph	2525 Observatory Ave.
Taylor, C. C.	Fairview & Madison Aves.
Thrasher, N. W.	3177 Linwood Rd.
Ustick, H. L.	2879 Erie Ave.
Updegrove, E. B.	1643 Brewster Ave.
Vogel, Wm. H.	3535 Fairview Ave.
Venable, Bryant	2482 Observatory Ave.
Volkman, A. C.	3415 Monteith Ave.
Voss, C. C.	Burch Ave.
Van Pyk, Prof. Tor	3547 Shaw Ave.
Weber, Dr. Charles	2615 Erie Ave.
Wright, J. Gano	2560 Observatory Ave.
Weis, John G.	3323 Monteith Ave.
Wright, Geo. L.	Station M.
Weitzel, Geo. L.	2786 Observatory Ave.
Weinheimer, Robert	2763 Madison Rd.
Woods, J. B.	3711 Drake Ave.
Wydman, Bryon S.	1330 Grace Ave.
Wuest, Mel. F.	2855 Madison Rd.
Winter, George	3560 Mooney Ave.
Weston, H. J.	2741 Observatory Ave.
Walsh, John M.	3570 Shaw Ave.
Witt, Michael	2920 Portsmouth Ave.
Woerz, Louis M.	2435 Madison Rd.
Wilson, Frank	3762 Isabella Ave.
Wetterman, Edward P.	319 Renson St., Reading, O.
Walton, Dr, Arthur P.	3607 Zumstein Ave,
Waltz, Chas. F.	2216 Kemper L., W. H.
Witte, C. Harvey	3528 Shaw Ave.
Weber, John	2826 Observatory Ave.
Wolker, J. M.	Madison Rd.
Wichert, Ernest	Dnncan Ave.
Williams, Robert E.	3555 Bolce Ave.
Walker, David A.	3723 Isabella Ave.
Widmeyer. W. W.	2872 Erie Ave.
Walters, Edward F.	Edwards & Erie Ave.
White, Jas. J., Jr	2849 Observatory Ave.
Wagner, John W.	3647 Edwards Rd.
Wohlmann, Wendel	Shady Lane.
Wood, John C.	2722 Madison Rd.
Weitzel, P. S.	Edwards & Erie Ave.
Wilson, Jos. A.	Observatory Rd.
Westing, Fred G.	2664 Madison Rd.
Williams, D. E.	1019 McMillan St.
Wurlitzer, R.	Madison & Bedford Aves.
Yoakley, John J.	3792 Oakley Ave.
Youmans, Fred M.	2612 Erie Ave.
Zucker, Charles C.	2773 Observatory Ave.
Zutterling, Al.	Brazee St., Oakley, O.
Zering, H.	N. E. Cor. Erie & Shady L
Ziegle, Louis E.	Paxton & Erie Aves.
Zettel, John	Menlo Ave.
Zeiner, Julius H.	2801 Madison Rd.

Grace Avenue Christian Church

In the fall of 1906 three persons interested in establishing a Church of Christ in Hyde Park, devoted to the restoration of the Christianity of the NEW TESTAMENT, purchased the building at the corner of Grace and Wilmer Aves., formerly occupied by the Baptist Church. At the close of a meeting held by Geo. P. Taubman in Jan. 1907, a church of 40 members was constituted with J. A. Lord, editor of the Christian Standard as minister, and regular sunday school and church services have been held ever since.

In April 1908, G. W. Thompson of the Richmond St. Christian Church held a good meeting. As a result of all these efforts the church membership is over fifty and the Sunday School has an enrollment of ninety.

The social life of the church is given emphasis, and strangers and visitors are made most welcome.

St. Mary's Catholic Church and School House

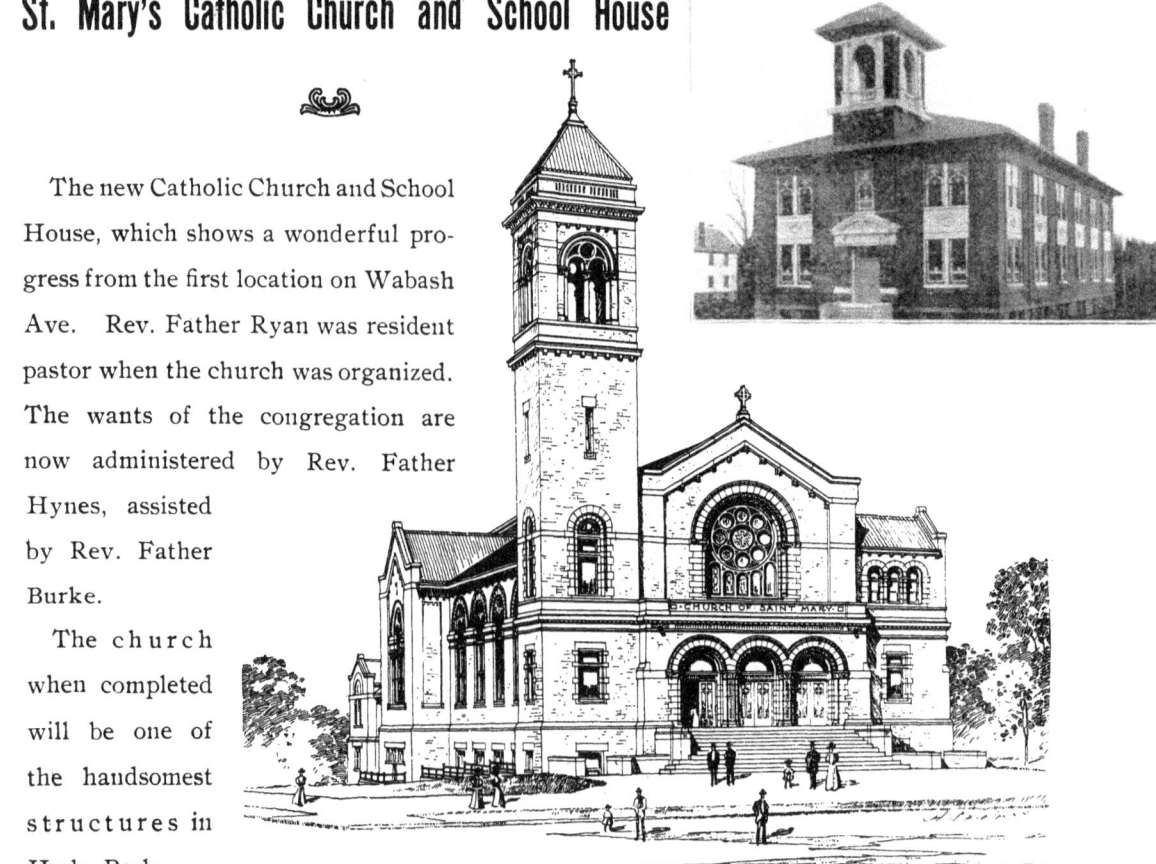

The new Catholic Church and School House, which shows a wonderful progress from the first location on Wabash Ave. Rev. Father Ryan was resident pastor when the church was organized. The wants of the congregation are now administered by Rev. Father Hynes, assisted by Rev. Father Burke.

The church when completed will be one of the handsomest structures in Hyde Park.

Knox Presbyterian Church

Shaw and Erie Ave.

Organized July 15, 1895

Rev. THEODORE T. HAYS, Pastor.
Residence: No. 3529 Michigan Ave.

Starting with three members in 1895 it now has 262 members and 340 children enrolled in the Sabbath School.

SERVICES:

SUNDAY
- Sabbath School - 9:30 a. m.
- Preaching - - - 11 a. m.
- Preaching - - - 7:45 p. m.

Wednesday - - - - 8 p. m.

All Welcome To All Services

Mt. Lookout M. E. Church

Cor. Observatory and Grace Aves.

This church was organized in the Spring of 1879 and this beautiful structure erected the following year and dedicated free of debt, December 5th, 1880.

The pastors officiating at and since the dedication have been Reverends E. T. Lane, Geo. M. Hammel, James Glasscock, Henry Witham, J. C. Heldt, J. H. Lease, John Gaddis, G. V. Morris and the present pastor O. P. Hoffman.

The church is in a flourishing condition with a membership of 211, Sept. 1st, 1907.

BAPTIST CHURCH, ERIE AND MICHIGAN AVES.

REV. JNO. MOSES LOCKHART, Res. 3516 St. Charles Pl.

The Hyde Park Baptist Church was organized January 20, 1790. At that time called Columbia; in 1827 name was changed to Duck Creek, and in 1904 took present name of Hyde Park.

This Church was the first Church in the North West territory, from the Ohio River to the Pacific Ocean.

AN HISTORICAL SKETCH

By "YE HISTORIAN."

The Burch Flats, Cor. Erie Ave. and Edwards Rd.

Hyde Park so picturesquely situated with its wide avenues, handsome homes and well kept lawns has rapidly excelled in beauty the many beautiful suburbs surrounding our home city of Cincinnati.

As the resident of Hyde Park returns to his home in this congenial and pleasant suburb, he has but one thought and that is that while doubtless the Creator could have made a more picturesque and beautiful suburb, it is also doubtless true, that he never has.

It is distinguished by the absence of characteristics which so often mar an otherwise beautiful suburb. Not a factory within it limits. Its streets broad and well kept. The homes all uniform and attractive. Its residents gathered to this green valley by the attraction of its beauty, its symetry, its location and the congenial and happy spirit of its fellow citizens. What is seen today is in many ways the outgrowth and result of many years of labor.

Twenty years ago Mornington was a familiar name, not only scattered around through our surrounding territory, but in every way one was constantly reminded by the quotation "Keep your eye on Mornington."

The Monteith Flats, Cor. Monteith and Observatory Aves.

Twenty-five or fifty inhabitants lived along its country roads, all of which were narrow, but some more narrow and winding than others, all mud, but some muddier than others. Not an unusual piece of architecture distinguished it from the ordinary farm grounds often seen adjacent to a large city. Its only means of transportation was the narrow gauge railroad, crossing above Edwards Road and Madison Pike, and the commuters who gathered on the wooden platform to take the morning

VIRGINIA FLATS, COR. ERIE AND MICHIGAN AVES.

A'LAISE FLAT BUILDING, COR. ERIE AVE. AND EDWARDS RD.

train, and returning in the evening were few.

The school house was a little red building at the corner of Edwards Road and Madison Pike still standing as an addition to our present commodious educational institution.

1892

About this time there gathered together a certain syndicate of wealthy, prosperous and patriotic citizens being Charles Kilgour, John Kilgour, James E. Mooney, Albert S. Berry, Wallace Burch, Simeon Johnson, John Zumstein and Thomas B.

RESIDENCE OF HON. L. E. ZIEGLE.

Youtsey, who formed what was then known as the Mornington Syndicate, purchasing almost all of the property in the triangle bounded by Edwards Road, Observatory Road and Madison Pike and a large stretch of ground to the east of Edwards Road. With the formation of the syndicate came the improvement of Madison Road, the street cars, the widening of Madison Road, first to the City limits and later to Oakley through the heart of the village, the building of Erie Avenue through the center of this farm ground under the direction of the County Commissioners, followed by

RESIDENCE OF DR. ARTHUR L. BROWN, ERIE AVE.

Mooney Avenue, Berry, Burch and Stettinius, the macadamizing, improvement and grading of Shaw Avenue through the ground then known as Shaw farm and Weber's woods.

This syndicate on the suggestion of Gustave W. Drach, changed name from Mornington to Hyde Park, and through their industry and perseverance is mainly due the fact that Hyde Park to-day is an exclusive residence district, protected, guarded and beautified by restrictions in the conveyance of property.

RESIDENCE OF JOHN B. SOKUP, ERIE AND MOONEY AVES.

The growth of Hyde Park for several years was not rapid, but the class of its improvement constantly attracted the attention and year by year it took a better and more commanding place among the home seekers of our City. It may be said here, that those restrictions and plans which were originally laid out by the Hyde Park Syndicate, for the developement of this section have been steadfastly adhered to, and it is mainly due to these restrictions, together with that careful scrutiny exercised in the sale of property, that the high class of citizenship in Hyde Park is now due.

In August, 1896 the

RESIDENCE OF ANDREW P. HENKEL, COR. MOONEY AND ERIE AVES.

first election for Village officials occurred. The incorporation of the Village only resulting after a bitter fight, and the first officials of the Village were Louis E. Zeigle, Mayor, Frank Johnson, Clerk, William F. Foy, Treasurer, John Kramer, Marshall, and the councilmen: William McCormick, Louis Bolce, William Kinkead, W. L. Voight, Dr. Clancey, R. C. Yowell, and W. J. Davidson, Solicitor.

The first village meeting was held in the room now occupied by the Hyde Park Savings Bank in the building at the corner of Edwards Road and Erie Avenue, and it was there that the Council was first organized. At the first election there were about two hundred and fifty votes cast, and to say that it was a hot election, is to put it mildly. But it is to this intense local feeling and the pride of each and every one in his home locality, that in a great measure contributes to the present local spirit so prevalent in our suburb. The candidates all made a house to house campaign. Their wives and children all electioneering, and the sole topic of conversation was the local issues then prevalent.

At the installation of these officials into their respective offices, Hyde

RESIDENCE OF M. Y. COOPER, 3590 MOONEY AVE.

RESIDENCE OF DR. R. K. PHILLIPS, ERIE AVE. AND EDWARDS RD.

Park was a community of very few residences, mud streets, few cement sidewalks, water pipes and gas only in a small portion of the locality, and with very poor street car facilities. The question of transportation by street cars to the City of Cincinnati was often then a more live topic of discussion than it is at the present time. Before the incorporation of the village the street cars had been extended first to O'Bryonsville, then to Observatory Road and from Observatory Road, for a short time, horse cars were run along the present route of Madison Road to Erie Avenue and Edwards Road.

RESIDENCE OF FRANK ANDREWS, SHAW AVE.

It was not long after the building of the street car line to Observatory Road before it was constructed through to Edwards Road and then to St. John's Park, but for many years thereafter, Hyde Park residents were contented with a jerky line of four cars running between St. John's Park and St. Francis de Sales Church. The only hope in those days was for an extension of the Cross Town line to Hyde Park, which would not have given direct connection with the City without transfer, but the rapid growth

RESIDENCE OF DR. AND MRS. CHAS. WEBER, 2615 ERIE AVE.

of the suburb even in those days convinced the street car authorities that the demands in that matter were less than what the people were entitled to, and thus was established the Madison Road car line, which exceeded in transportation facilities the most extravagant wishes of the residents at that time.

Hyde Park as a village, can be proud of many of its accomplishments, as street improvements, extension of water, gas and sewers, the building of the Town Hall, the erection of the fountain and many other improvements were made.

RESIDENCE OF W. H. CLEMONS, 2623 ERIE AVE.

But more than that can be said of Hyde Park, as a village, for during the whole of its official life not an official of the Village nor an official act of any of the officials, was ever condemned on account of corruption. No matter how high and wealthy the individual was, he was willing and anxious to accept the duties of any office and all duties were faithfully and honestly performed. The three mayors of the Village were Louis E. Ziegle, G. F. Osler and Wm. J. McCormick.

While Hyde Park has its three marshalls

RESIDENCE OF N. J. WALSH, EDWARDS ROAD

and its prison, during the whole official life of the Village but one arrest was ever made, and that was but a short time before the annexation to the City, and a non-resident at that, the offense being disorderly conduct.

RESIDENCE OF W. L. SPIEGEL, ERIE AVE.

THE PINES
RESIDENCE OF JOHN KILGOUR, ERIE AVE.

RESIDENCE OF MRS. I. E. HALL.

THE residence and grounds of Mrs. I. E. Hall, located at the N. W. Corner of Shaw and Wabash Avenues. The house is built of stone and concrete while the ample grounds are abundantly shaded.

The Hall home contributes to the general air of refinement that distinguishes this residence section of Hyde Park.

THE artistic home of John W. Lee, 3571 Mooney Avenue.

Mr. Lee has given much personal attention to beautifying the grounds with numerous varieties of foliage, which will convert this original home into a land of verdure.

RESIDENCE OF JNO. W. LEE, 3571 MOONEY AVE.

RESIDENCE OF FRANK O. SUIRE, BERRY AVE.

This residence, while not one of those most recently erected, yet, by reason of its substantial construction, and the various embellishments and improvements that have been added, fairly represents the homelike and comfortable character of the residences in what was formerly the village of Hyde Park.

This is a picture of the residence of Judge Wm. Littleford, on Salem Avenue, in Hyde Park. The grounds have an artistic arrangement of flower beds, in which are grown nearly all kinds of hardy and annual flowers, while the vegetable garden and hot beds contain almost every vegetable known to this climate. In addition to his extensive and beautifully kept grounds, the Judge is a fancier of Jersey cows, pigeons and chickens.

RESIDENCE OF JUDGE WM. LITTLEFORD.

This cut exhibits the home of M. F. Galvin, of the law firm of Galvin & Bauer. It was the first house built on Stettinius Ave., twelve years ago by Louis Goldkamp, the builder, for himself; and sold five years ago to Mr. Galvin. It consists of eleven rooms, the lower floor finished in light straw-colored oak, and the upper rooms in carefully selected curly pine.

The location is protected against the construction of all business houses as well as cheap dwellings, which makes it the most exclusive residential district in Hyde Park.

RESIDENCE OF M. F. GALVIN.

RESIDENCE OF DR. C. G. FOERTMEYER, GRADUATE PHYSICIAN AND DRUGGIST, 3562 SHAW AVE.

The imposing Colonial dwelling at 3562 Shaw Ave., was constructed a year ago for the owner, Dr. C. G. Foertmeyer. Nothing is absent that could enhance comfort or elegance. The terraced grounds with winding driveway combine to produce one of Hyde Park's most inviting homes.

THE OBSERVATORY
OBSERVATORY PLACE

HYDE PARK
PUBLIC SCHOOL

SHADY LANE AND ERIE AVENUE

ERIE AVENUE, EAST OF SHAW

THE PUBLIC SQUARE

J. J. SULLIVAN & CO.
AT ERIE AVE., OPP. MICHIGAN

HYDE PARK BUSINESS CLUB EXCURSION TO NEW WATER WORKS

What Subject Interests You Most?

No matter what line of reading you follow you will find in our large book stock many of the latest and best works on that subject. And, what is more important, in charge of that book stock you will find men whose wide knowledge of the book market enables them to render you valuable assistance in the choice of your reading.

Are you interested in any of these subjects? Come examine our stock of books; any or all of them.

Automobiling	Elocution	Photography
Art	Essays	Pedagogy
Arts and Crafts	Fiction	Poetry
Architecture	Gardening	Philosophy
Advertising	Gift Books	Psychology
Biography	Horticulture	Physical Culture
Cooking	History	Sociology
Collecting	Juvenile	Travel
Drama	Music	Theology
Devotional	Nature	

JENNINGS & GRAHAM
The Western Methodist Book Concern
220 WEST FOURTH STREET

HOW MUCH DOES IT COST?

Is a question asked by every careful buyer, and if the article costs more at one store than at another, the store which charges the higher prices is not patronized. Ask this same question when buying life insurance and investigate for yourself, and you will find that the company which insures at the lowest cost and returns the largest amount on Endowment Policies is the

Union Central Life
Insurance Company of Cincinnati.

ASSETS $62,000,000   ESTABLISHED 1867

JESSE R. CLARK, Pres.   E. P. MARSHALL, V. Pres.
E. W. JEWELL, General Agent for Cincinnati.

MICHIE BROTHERS
DIAMONDS, WATCHES AND JEWELRY
MANUFACTURING JEWELERS

Telephone 699.   Factory: No. 408 Home Street.

212 West Fourth St.   CINCINNATI, O.

LAW OFFICES OF
WILLIAW LITTLEFORD
FIRST NATIONAL BANK BUILDING
CINCINNATI

HENRY G. FROST   AMOS P. FOSTER

Established 1884.

W. J. MUNSTER
Certified Public Accountant

315 Carlisle Building

Tel. Main 2762   CINCINNATI

L. REDLER
Manufacturing FURRIER
and Importer

640 Race St., Opp. Shillitos   CINCINNATI, O.

Louis H. Bolce & Company

Manufacturers of

PAINTS

AND

COLORS

Calcimo Tints

FOR

Walls and Ceilings

LOUIS H. BOLCE
The LINSEED OIL Man.

Dealers in

Painters' Supplies

Liquid Veneer and Jap=a=lac

...JOBBERS OF...

LINSEED OIL AND WINDOW GLASS

Special REMOVAL notice!   Note the date! January 1, 1909

We will move into our new fire-proof building which will be built on our lots Nos. 2425-2427-2429 Gilbert Ave., near Peebles Corner, and what will be known in the future as **"Jones' Square"** when the widening of Gilbert Avenue is completed.

You-needa paints, and You-No-It.

    We-needa money, and We-No-It.

        Let us make an even trade.

N. B.—We are still located at the "OLD STAND" 2311-2313 Gilbert Avenue, and our TELEPHONE number is NORTH 428.

......Of course, we deliver the goods.

"COLUMBIA IDEAL" POLICIES

Protection for Your Family; Provision for Your Old Age.

A postal card TODAY may save YOUR widow from want, your house from the mortgage, your children from the asylum, and yourself from the infirmary.

Send address, age and occupation to the

The Columbia Life Insurance Co.

W. C. CULKINS, General Manager.

RAWSON BUILDING, - - CINCINNATI, OHIO

The Hyde Park Lumber Co.

Madison Road and N. & W. Ry.

TELEPHONE EAST 203

- Covers six acres of factory space
- Capacity a house a day
- Furnishes millwork, rough and dressed lumber
- A complete stock of house building material ready for immediate shipment
- Also manufactures and builds complete stair sets
- Estimates cheerfully furnished

THE VICTOR

Burglar proof Bank Safes, Vaults and Deposit Boxes.

Fire proof Safes and Boxes.

The Victor Safe & Lock Co.,
CINCINNATI, OHIO.

GILBERT & PIPER
...Real Estate Brokers...

Make a Specialty of Hyde Park Property

The Only Real Estate Office in Hyde Park

List With Us for Quick Results

Offices in the Betz Bldg.   Tel. East 462

For 🌼 🌼 🌼

Pictures, Picture Framing
Kodak, Kodak Supplies
and Wood to Burn

...SEE...

HUBER'S   603 Race St.

HERBERT T. KENT   AUGUST J. KAUFHOLD

Kent & Kaufhold
...BROKERS...

Real Estate, Loans and Investments
Rents Collected

Office, 809 Mercantile Library Bldg.

Phone Main 222.   CINCINNATI, OHIO

S. W. McGRATH, Pres.   J. H. DIERKES, V. Pres.

Cincinnati Fly Screen Co.
...Manufacturers of...

CINCINNATI RUSTLESS SCREENS

8th and Evans Street,   -   -   CINCINNATI, OHIO

EDWARD G. SCHULTZ　　　　　JOHN C. FROHLIGER
Res. Phone W. 2511-X　　　　Res. Phone East 129-Y

PHONE CANAL 4432

AUDITING　　SYSTEMATIZING　　ACCOUNTING

Schultz & Frohliger,

PUBLIC ACCOUNTANTS

and Manufacturers of

Loose Leaf Devices

111 E. Sixth St.,　　- -　　CINCINNATI, O.

Folding Chairs　　　　　　　　　*Carriages*

W. D. Jacocks & Co.

PRIVATE AMBULANCE

Funeral Directors and Licensed Embalmers

PHONES:
Office, N. 1465
Residence, N. 1838-Y

2447 Gilbert Ave., W. H.　　CINCINNATI

W. T. McLEAN, A. M., M. D., D. D. S.

Surgical and Prosthetic

DENTISTRY

a Specialty

104 W. Fourth St.　　Tel. Main 4357
N. W. Cor. 4th and Race

OFFICE: 400 Neave Building

HOURS:
9 to 12 A. M.
2 to 6 P. M.　　CINCINNATI, O.

Allan Ross Raff

BUILDER'S SUPPLIES

REPRESENTING:
Celadon Roofing Tile Co.
Columbus Brick and Terra Cotta Co.
The Ironclay Brick Co.
White Limestone, Metal Lath and Wall Ties.
North Eastern Terra Cotta Co.
Kittanning Brick and Fire Clay Co.
The Chamberlain Metal Weather Strip Co.

Room 43, Mitchell Building,

Telephone, 4151-X

No. 9 W. Fourth St,　　　　CINCINNATI.

FRED. H. LINGONNER
REAL ESTATE

Builder   Fire Insurance

3742 Oakley Avenue
Phone, Elm 92-R

HYDE PARK,   CINCINNATI

WM. B. BARR
Carpenter and Builder

Special Attention Given to all Kinds of Repairing

Tel. Canal 250.

805-807 BROADWAY,   **CINCINNATI**

G. L. MELLOR   Tel. East 417   E. F. MELLOR

MELLOR BROS.
PLUMBING AND GAS FITTING

Modern Plumbing a Specialty   Hot Water Heating and Gas Appliances

ERIE AVE. and EDWARDS RD. - - CINCINNATI, O.

JOHN STRIKER
Tailor

406 Main Street   *CINCINNATI, O.*

Furniture of Quality

CHARACTER AND PRICE
Have Distinguished this House as the Leader in Good Furniture.

C. & A. KREIMER 907-915 Main St.

Richard G. Bray
...BROKER...
And Dealer in High Grade Stocks and Bonds

Cincinnati Street Ry.	6% stock
Cincinnati Gas & Electric	5% "
C. N. & C. Preferred	4½% "
Cincinnati Bell Telephone Co.	8% "
Procter & Gamble Co.	12% "

Member of Cincinnati Stock Exchange.

212-213 Fourth Nat. Bank Bldg.
TELEPHONE M. 3257.

E. F. Walter

Wholesale and Retail

Baker, Confectioner and Caterer

Fine Candies and Creams

Special Attention Given to Private Parties, Weddings, Etc.

MAIN OFFICE, Edwards and Erie Aves.

BAKERY, Cor. Monteith and Observatory Aves.

PHONES: { East 315-R. / East 111-X. / East 67 Orders Only. } **Hyde Park**

WEITZEL'S MARKET

"Good Things To Eat"

N. E. Cor. Erie Ave. and Edwards Rd.
Telephones East 180 and 426

HYDE PARK. CINCINNATI, O.

The Charles E. Smith Sons Co.

HAVE PLEASED MANY THOUSANDS OF MEN

... BY SUPPLYING ...

GOOD SHIRTS AT MODEST PRICES

MEN'S FURNISHING GOODS

FORTY-NINE EAST FOURTH ST.

LOUIS E. ZIEGLE, President   MYERS Y. COOPER, Vice-President   EDMUND G. COOK, Sec'y-Treas.

A FIRE ENGINE COMPANY PROTECTS THE COMMUNITY
A BANK ACCOUNT PROTECTS THE INDIVIDUAL

The Hyde Park Savings Bank

PAYS THREE PER CENT. INTEREST ON SAVINGS DEPOSITS

... AND ...

RESPECTFULLY SOLICITS

YOUR COMMERCIAL OR CHECKING ACCOUNT

BANKING ROOM—PUBLIC SQUARE

THIS is the mattress that shows you what's inside.

It is the quality of the Cotton used and the way they are made that give Stearns & Foster Mattresses their perfect comfort and wonderful life.

A positive guarantee on every mattress.

ON SALE AT ALL REPUTABLE FURNITURE AND DEPARTMENT STORES.

The Stearns & Foster Co.,
CINCINNATI, - - O.

Photographs In This Book By

Edward M. Scheid

COMMERCIAL PHOTOGRAPHER

44 ARCADE, CINCINNATI, O.

ENLARGEMENTS: Any Body - Any Time - Any Thing - Any Place.

Producer of Fine Photographs   **PHONE Main 5146-R**

CAPITAL, - $1,000,000

THE HYDE PARK BUILDING AND LOAN CO.

Meets Every Saturday Night in Betz Building,
Cor. Erie and Edwards Road

Shares 50c.   No Initiation.

ACCOUNTS SOLICITED.
MONEY TO LOAN.

Established in 1894, since which time we have never had any litigation nor any loss of any character.

OFFICERS.

Jas. E. Sherwood, Pres.	Geo. N. Brown, V. Pres.
G. Green, Sec'y.	E. F. Walter, Treas.

Finance Committee: { Christ. Stichnath. Frank Robertson, Ass't Sec'y. A. C. Volkman.

F. H. Kinney.	Edward Cordes.	Andrew J. Murphy.
M. J. Flynn.		Julius G. Penn, Att'y.

We sell Coal in Hyde Park.

It's real clean Coal that Krogers sell,
It does not smoke or make a smell,
It does not dirty your cellar I tell,
But makes a heat—that's worse than H—.

KROGER COAL & COKE CO.

Main Office:

34 Mitchell Building, 9 West Fourth Street.

Hill Top Yard:

Shillito Street and C. L. & N. Ry.

Telephones: Main 671; Main 672; North 958

LOUIS E. KUHLER, Salesman

Telephone E. 315-L.

ANTHRACITE, YOUGHIOGHENY, KANAWHA, POCAHONTAS, COKE.

MURPHY & DITCHEN

...MODERN PLUMBERS...

Plumbing in all its branches

Special attention given to Natural Gas Fittings

WASSON and EDWARDS RD.   Telephone East. 416

FOERTMEYER'S

PHARMACY

N. E. Cor. 6th & Central Ave.   CINCINNATI, OHIO

FRANK WILSON

Merchant Tailor   ❧ ❧ ❧   FRENCH DRYING, DRY CLEANING
                                      REPAIRING AND ALTERATIONS

VIRGINIA BUILDING, ERIE AND MICHIGAN AVES.

"FROM FACTORY TO FIRESIDE"
HARDWOOD FLOORS
PLAIN AND ORNAMENTAL
CINCINNATI FLOOR CO.
...MANUFACTURERS...

PHONE, M. 3343.   228 WEST FOURTH ST.

Delicious Soda.   Fine Cigars.

THINK IT OVER

When you want DRUGS or a Prescription filled you want Good, Pure, Fresh Goods Only!

YOU WANT IT RIGHT and at City Prices.

—— All To Be Had At ——

THE VIRGINIA PHARMACY

W. W. FORD, Mgr.

Cor. Erie and Michigan Aves.

Opp. Town Hall,   HYDE PARK

TELEPHONE E. 456.

We carry a fine line of Candies, Toilet Articles, Nursery Supplies, Stationery, Etc., Etc.

Courteous Attention   Prompt Delivery.

The Hyde Park Supply Company

Madison Road and N. & W. R. R.

Telephone Elm 715.

—— DEALERS IN ——

High Grade Coal

For Furnace and Range Use.

Also largest Stock Brick Manufacturers in Hamilton County.

—— DEALERS IN ——

BUILDERS' SUPPLIES

Real Estate Bought and Sold.   Ground Rents Bought and Sold.   Estates Managed.
Rents Collected.   Loans Negotiated.   Collections Made.

Richard B. Cadwalader
..Real Estate and Loans..

405=6 Johnston Bldg.,   PHONES: { Office, M. 1630 / Residence, E. 794-R. }   Cincinnati, Ohio

IF YOU WANT HYDE PARK

Improved or Vacant Property

IT WILL PAY YOU TO SEE

MYERS Y. COOPER

UNION TRUST BUILDING

Telephones Main 2213-2214

America's Pride.

The world's best table water.

"WHITE ROCK"

Always be loyal to home pro= ductions; where merit justifies.

Wilmot J. Hall

Distributor.

The words "French Bros." used on the label on ice cream and milk iusure an article of the highest merit.

The French Bros. Ice Cream is of the most delicious flavor, smooth and nutritious.

Milk and Cream furnished by this firm represent the acme of the dairymen's success.

FRENCH BROS.

316-318 W. 7th St.

TELEPHONE CANAL 489.

And now a word in closing—when your Publicity Committee was appointed, we were informed that we were appointed to not only make our Hyde Park Business Club well and favorably known, but to spread the glories of Hyde Park as a suburb far and wide. How well we have succeeded the reader can best judge. The Committee desires to call attention to the advertisers and ask your favorable consideration of their propositions.

We wish to express our sincere thanks to all those who have helped to make this booklet possible.

The Publicity Committee:

R. E. MORRISON, *Chairman*, M. J. FLYNN, C. HARVEY WITTE.

Van's Improved Family Steel Ranges
For Coal or Natural Gas

The Best Bakers.   **Greatest Coal Savers.**   **Every Range Guaranteed.**

Gas Ranges, Refrigerators and all kinds of Culinary Implements.

The John Van Range Co. - - 5th and Broadway
Cincinnati, · · · Ohio

www.ingramcontent.com/pod-product-compliance
Lightning Source LLC
Chambersburg PA
CBHW051809100526
44592CB00016B/2626